Edith Matilda Thomas

Lyrics and Sonnets

Edith Matilda Thomas

Lyrics and Sonnets

ISBN/EAN: 9783744796200

Printed in Europe, USA, Canada, Australia, Japan

Cover: Foto ©Thomas Meinert / pixelio.de

More available books at **www.hansebooks.com**

LYRICS AND SONNETS

BY

EDITH M. THOMAS

AUTHOR OF "A NEW YEAR'S MASQUE AND OTHER POEMS"

BOSTON AND NEW YORK
HOUGHTON, MIFFLIN AND COMPANY
The Riverside Press, Cambridge
1887

By EDITH M. THOMAS.

All rights

The Riverside Press, Cambridge:
Electrotyped and Printed by H. O. Houghton & Co.

TO MY DEAR MOTHER.

Thou smilest that my childhood's dreaming thought
So blent thee with the beauty of God's world
That those deep morning lilies dew-impearled,
And jonquils clear with vernal wildness fraught
(In the old lost garden where thy hand had wrought),
And dove-plumes of an evening cloud soft curled,
And star-sheen to the bland night wind unfurled,
Some touch of thy fair tenderness had caught.
Later the world of all things excellent,
As once of lovely, moved round thee ; and still
Whene'er I hear the praise of Truth, Good-Will,
High Hope, and Courage by no tempest bent,
I can but think these names for thee were meant,
And thou art Love, else hath my heart no skill !

CONTENTS.

LYRICS.

SONNETS.

LYRICS.

THE BREATHING EARTH.

Oh, not by sight or sound alone, I guess
   This way her light feet press, —
     Light feet of Spring!

It would be told me, though I shut my eyes
   Against the ample sky's
     Pure witnessing,
And saw not how the green blade thrusts its way
   Up through the pleachèd gray, —
     No tenderling!
It would be told me, though I shut my ear
   To all the tidings clear
     Her heralds bring, —
The fluting thrush, the bluebird singing love,
   Hiding in heaven above
     His heaven-dyed wing.

How, sight and sound shut out, should I still guess
   This way her light feet press, —
     Light feet of Spring?

(11)

By errantry of subtile winds that blow
   From fields where late the snow
      Did drift and cling;
By grateful odors borne from forest mold,
   Where last year's leaves enfold
      Some blooming thing;
By healing essence, lifeful airs, unbound
   From the dark, humid ground
      Fast mellowing,
Whence, from the smoking, furrowed clods, still come
   The gnats with ceaseless hum
      And hovering.

The breathing earth!   I breathe, and well I guess
   This way her light feet press, —
      Light feet of Spring!

THE DREAMER.

OH, not for her the early violet,
The swarm-like buds upon the fruit-trees set,
The robin singing in the first Spring rain.
She will have gone ere these can come again.

And therefore is it that soft, pitying Sleep,
Each night, by ways the Winter cannot keep,
Brings her where bloom the flowers her childhood knew
In griefless places kissed by sun and dew.

(13)

SNOWDROPS.

In snowdrops, well I ween,
A loving-cup is seen,
A pledge betwixt soft Spring
And the frore-bearded King;
For see ! the chalice shows
White as the Winter's snows,
Save, here, brim-stains of green ;
'T is plain what these should mean, —
So many times the lip
Of Spring did touch and sip.

(14)

ANEMONE.

" THOU faintly blushing, dawn-like bloom
    That springest on the April path,
Set round with shivering leafy gloom
    'Mong thy companions frail and rath,
Why spurnest thou the golden sun,
    Whom all with still delight receive?
Some unknown love thy heart hath won,
    And whispers thee at morn and eve!
How may this be, how may this be,
    O rare Anemone?"

" The wind my sunshine is; the wind,
    That many a trembling flower affrays,
Alone my sweetness can unbind,
    Alone my drooping eye upraise.
And when my thread of life shall break,
    And when I cast my raiment white,
Me gently will the rough wind take
    And bear along his boundless flight.
He calleth me, — ' Be free, be free,
    My own Anemone!' "

(15)

VALENTINE.

IF thou canst make the frost be gone,
  And fleet away the snow
  (And that thou canst, I trow) ;
If thou canst make the Spring to dawn,
Hawthorn to put her brav'ry on,
Willow, her weeds of fine green lawn,
    Say why thou dost not so —
        Aye, aye !
      Say why
    Thou dost not so !

If thou canst chase the stormy rack,
  And bid the soft winds blow
  (And that thou canst, I trow) ;
If thou canst call the thrushes back
To give the groves the songs they lack,
And wake the violet in thy track, —
    Say why thou dost not so —
        Aye, aye !
      Say why
    Thou dost not so !

If thou canst make my Winter Spring,
  With one word breathèd low
  (And that thou canst, I know) ;

If, in the closure of a ring,
Thou canst to me such treasure bring,
My state shall be above a king,
   Say why thou dost not so —
      Aye, aye !
      Say why
    Thou dost not so !

THE HEART'S CALL.

He rides away at early light,
   Amid the tingling frost,
And in the mist that sweeps her sight
   His form is quickly lost.

He crosses now the silent stream,
   Now skirts the forest drear,
Whose thickets cast a silver gleam
   From leafage thin and sear.

Long falls the shadow at his back
   (The morning springs before);
His thoughts fly down the shadowed track,
   And haunt his cottage-door.

Miles gone, upon a hilltop bare
   He draws a sudden rein:
His name, her voice, rings on the air,
   Then all is still again!

She sits at home, she speaks no word,
   But deeply calls her heart;
And this it is that he has heard,
   Though they are miles apart.

THE BLUEBIRD.

SOMETIME in Heaven sojourned this bird,
And there the chant of the seraphs heard ;
One note of the theme it repeateth still —
" Cherish, cherish, oh ! cherish " — till
Quivers the song-swept blue above ;
   And earth, lying dreamily under,
   Thrills with delight and wonder —
     " Cherish Love."

Therefore the bloom to the apple-bough,
The flower to the wood-knoll, springeth now,
And leaf-mist gathers in copse and glen.
" Cherish, cherish, oh ! cherish," again
The flute-voice calls from the blue above.
   How shall I dare gainsay it ?
   What should I do but obey it ?
     " Cherish Love."

Not now can the seed be pent underground,
The bud in its Winter sheath be bound,
Nor the spirit in me be chained and dark.
" Cherish, cherish, oh ! cherish " — hark
To the seraph-taught in the blue above !
   But if the song should not reach thee,
   Who shall it be that will teach thee
     " Cherish Love " ?

LEFT OUT.

OVER parchèd hill and plain
Sweep the legions of the rain.
Here its bounty knows no stay,
Here in showers it ebbs away,
Here unslaked the summer burns ;
Downward to the mother turns
Choicest flower of all the fields,
With a sigh its spirit yields.
You may blame the rain or no,
But it ever hath been so :
Something loveliest of its race
Perisheth from out its place,
For the lack of freshening care,
While the rain pours otherwhere.

From the caverned shores and seas
Springs the wafting sail-loved breeze ;
To its port speeds many a bark,
Like an arrow to the mark.
Here a zephyr's might it blows,
Here the sea unruffled flows ;
Here is held with sails asleep
Swiftest ship that swept the deep.

You may blame the wind or no,
But it ever hath been so :
Something bravest of its kind
Leads a frustrate life and blind,
For the lack of favoring gales,
Blowing blithe on other sails.

SPIRIT TO SPIRIT.

DEAD? Not to thee, thou keen watcher, — not silent,
  not viewless, to thee,
Immortal still wrapped in the mortal! I, from the
  mortal set free,
Greet thee by many clear tokens thou smilest to hear
  and to see.

For I, when thou wakest at dawn, to thee am the enter-
  ing morn;
And I, when thou walkest abroad, am the dew on the
  leaf and the thorn,
The tremulous glow of the noon, the twilight on harvests of corn.

I am the flower by the wood-path, — thou bendest to
  look in my eyes;
The bird in its nest in the thicket, — thou heedest my
  love-laden cries;
The planet that leads the night legions, — thou liftest
  thy gaze to the skies.

And I am the soft-dropping rain, the snow with its
  fluttering swarms;

The summer-day cloud on the hilltops, that showeth
    thee manifold forms;
The wind from the south and the west, the voice that
    sings courage in storms!

Sweet was the earth to thee ever, but sweeter by far to
    thee now:
How hast thou room for tears, when all times marvelest
    thou,
Beholding who dwells with God in the blossoming
    sward and the bough!

Once as a wall were the mountains, once darkened
    between us the sea;
No longer these thwart and baffle, forbidding my pas-
    sage to thee:
Immortal still wrapped in the mortal, I linger till thou
    art set free!

AT DEATH'S DOOR.

BELOVÈD, thou wouldst question me
What things the parting soul doth see.

That moment of the still, gray prime
When, fleeing from the house of time,

The spirit through mine eyelids passed
(Thy kisses sealed those windows last),

I touched, obscure, a threshold stone,
A Door I reached, spent and alone.

All void before, my spirit then
Turned on the past its doubtful ken.

Along the road I had o'ergone,
A tenfold light began to dawn.

Each day of life revealèd stood,
Each with its dower of ill or good ;

And deed, and thought, and flitting dream,
Showed clear as mote in sunny beam.

(24)

On every scene mine eyes had known,
The sudden splendor flashed and shone:

The woodland places, dim and sweet,
Wherein I set my childish feet;

The evening hearth, the candle-light,
Far beckoning down the Winter night;

The dark, unmeasured, rushing sea,
And youth's wild joy of being free!

The alien city's solitude,
Its paven ways, its turmoil rude.

Uprose each face of friend or foe,
Or stranger's, chance-met long ago —

The swift reproach, the look askance,
The laughing gaze, the heart-warm glance!

All hours of life! but last the hour
I name for thee and for love's power!

Then earthward light and vision died,
And the great Door swung still and wide.

What then I saw transcends thy speech:
Its name in Heaven how can I teach!

ON EASTER MORN.

I HAD not known that I was dead,
Until I heard it softly said
By the quick grass above my head,
And by the many-budded thorn,
  On Easter morn.

"Yea, thou art dead" (these whispered me), —
"Dead long ago; none seeketh thee;
Thy sealèd eyes shall never see
The Lord of Life put death to scorn
  On Easter morn."

I said, "One thing deny me not:
With all your bloom and verdure plot
To make my grave the fairest spot
That by His footsteps shall be worn
  On Easter morn."

Then in the dim and sighing hour
Ere over darkness light hath power,
They wrought together — blade and flower —
The mould above me to adorn
  For Easter morn.

I felt His footsteps pause and stay,
Felt the sweet, searching light of day.
" Rise, grateful dust ! " I heard Him say ;
" For thee have I put death to scorn
     On Easter morn."

SEA-BIRD AND LAND-BIRD.

A LAND-BIRD would follow a sea-bird's flight
Over the surges and out of sight.
    It joyed to lave
    In the bead of the wave,
And watch the great sky in its mirror glassed;
    And all was well
    Till, with measureless swell,
Under the gale rose the waters vast.
    Then, baffled and maimed,
    With spirit tamed,
The bird 'mid the drift on the shore was cast.

Thou wast that sea-bird strong and light
(Shall a land-bird follow a sea-bird's flight?) —
    Wast fledged on high,
    Close under the sky;
The wandering cloud would sometimes bend
    With billowy breast
    Above thy nest,
And in pity moist her substance spend;
    No mate thou couldst find
    Like the fierce North Wind,
And the tempest that tried thee most was thy friend!

I was that land-bird, frail and slight
(Shall a sea-bird stay for a land-bird's flight?);
    Low on the earth
    I had my birth,
In a sunny field where the days were long;
    There, as I lay,
    I heard the spray
Of the grass in June growing deep and strong;
    Fast the days flew,
    And I followed, too;
And saluted the sun with my slender song!

Hear me, thou sea-bird, matchless in flight,
Shaping thy course o'er the surges white!
    In the making of things,
    Strength fell to thy wings,
So that thou shouldst not falter nor tire
    When beating abroad;
    The breath of a god
Was breathed through thy form, — an enduring fire:
    To me, out of heaven,
    No fire was given,
Nor strength, but only the rover's desire!

Shall a land-bird follow a sea-bird's flight
Over the surges and out of sight?
    The Maker of things
    Has touched my wings,
And taken from me my blind unrest!
    Now am I blent
    With the fields' content,

In the grassy deep where I make my nest. —
  Say, canst thou hear
  My carol clear, —
Thou, by the soundful sea oppressed?

FRAILTY'S SHIELD.

Look what arms the fenceless wield, —
Frailest things have frailty's shield !
Cockle-boat outrides the gale
That has shred the frigate's sail ;
Curlew skims the breaker's crest ;
Swings the oriole in its nest ;
Flower a single summer bred
Lightly lifts its jaunty head,
When is past the storm whose stroke
Laid the pride of centuried oak ;
Where with fire the soil was bathed
The white trefoil springs unscathed.

Frailest things have frailty's shield :
Here a fly in amber sealed ;
There a bauble, tossed aside
Under ancient lava-tide,
Meets the musing delver's gaze.
Time the king's memorial lays,
Touching it with sportive staff,
But spares Erotion's epitaph.

Frailest things have frailty's shield,
Guarded by a charm concealed ;

So the gaunt and ravening wild
Softens towards the weaning child,
And along the giddy steep
Safe one glideth, blind with sleep.

Art thou mighty ? — Challenged Fate
Chooseth thee for wrestling mate !
Art thou feeble ? — Fate disarmed,
Turning, leaveth thee unharmed.
Thou that bendest shalt not break ;
Smiling in the tempest's wake,
Thou shalt rise, and see around
How the strong ones strew the ground ;
Saving lightness thou didst wield, —
Frailest things have frailty's shield !

THE SHORE WITHOUT A PORT.

I KNOW a shore without a port, —
'T were better be the east wind's sport
　　Than to adventure here!
Sails drooped and motionless, we stand
Not more than one poor league from land,
　　Yet thither may not steer.

Such calm prevails, 't were not more vain,
Shipmates, upon the waveless plain
　　To give the sail and oar.
Like flickering metal cooled in mold,
A solid sea of burnished gold
　　Divides us from the shore.

The land is fair and flowerful:
On many an old-wrecked, floating hull,
　　Wing'd seeds, windblown, alight;
They spring again in rank display, —
The lotus, kissed with sun and spray,
　　And unknown flowers of night.

Good sooth! an idle crew are we
To have no errand on the sea,
　　No trade with any strand:

(33)

We nothing do but strive to guess
(With lids half-shut in idleness)
    What shapes are on the land.

Some say this region is the home
Of elf, and sprite, and urchin gnome,
    A shrewd and jealous clan ;
And some have seen a gala rout
Of Loves and Graces borne about
    In Cytherea's van.

But some, of holier vision, deem
This is the seat of every dream
    The gods send dreaming youth :
Our crew is like to mutiny,
No two the same delight can see,
    Yet each contends for Truth !

GRAY HAIR IN YOUTH.

WHAT does youth with silvered crown?
Snows of winter come not down
Till the frost hath made its way,
And the night outmeasured day;
Till the harvest all is stored,
And the cordial vintage poured
That can heavy memories drown.
What does youth with silvered crown?

Passion's fires have burned apace,
Laying waste the summer's grace,
Than the frost more cruel keen,
Making youth as age be seen,
Save upon his silken hairs
Ashes white, not snow, he bears, —
Mournful frame for morning face!
Passion's fires have burned apace.

PONCE DE LEON.

You that crossed the ocean old,
Not from greed of Inca's gold.
But to search by vale and mount,
Wood and rock, the wizard fount
Where Time's harm is well undone, —
Here 's to Ponce de Leon,
And your liegemen every one!
Surely, still beneath the sun,
In some region further west,
You live on and have your rest,
While the world goes spinning round,
And the sky hears the resound
Of a thousand shrill new fames,
Which your jovial silence shames!
Strength and joy your days endow,
Youth's eyes glow beneath your brow;
Wars and vigils are forgot,
And the Scytheman threats you not.
Tell us, of your knightly grace,
Tell us, left you not some trace
Leading to that wellspring true
Where old souls their age renew?

THE HEART UPON THE SLEEVE.

WHAT, noble masters, all amort?
Why will ye be the mob-world's sport,
And let each knave his weapon pick
Wherewith to stab ye to the quick!

Lo! arms and charms ye do not lack
(If arms and charms could save from wrack),
Nor any point of crafty art
To triple fence and guard the heart!

Yet ye are scathed; unhurt am I,
Though to attack I open lie:
All nude of corselet, casque, or greave,
I wear my heart upon my sleeve!

Since on the day Truth's lips I kissed,
No hest of hers could I resist;
She turns and winds me at her will,
Her lips set mine the copy still.

She will not let me doubt or shrink
To roundly speak what I must think;
She lays this charge upon my skill,
To part entwining Good and Ill.

My heart upon my sleeve I wear,
And all who see may read it there ;
"That poor, plain thing. a heart ? " they cry,
And subtle-minded pass it by.

I laugh, I sigh, I praise, I chide,
With moods of mirth and sadness pied ;
They call me. then. chameleon elf
That hath no color of himself.

But some, suspecting artifice,
The life they seek to take still miss,
Since all the deeper they may smite,
I bear my heart more high and light!

They think I case my bosom frail
With woven links of hidden mail ;
The simple truth will none believe, —
I wear my heart upon my sleeve!

Still, noble masters, all amort?
Your shields, your plates of proof, fall short;
But wear the heart upon the sleeve,
And not a dint shall it receive !

THE PALMER.

THOU who wouldst a palmer be,
Let thy faith suffice to thee.
Say not, " I to-morrow will
Get beyond the sunrise hill,
Pass the sea, and cross the sand
Till I come to Holy Land,
And beneath the lamps that glow
In the shrine my heart I show,
Leave my gift and round my vow,
Bearing thence the victor bough."

Say not this, nor take in hand
Staff and scrip for Holy Land.
Thou be wiser than the rest
Who have bound them to the quest;
Breathe thy vow and waft thy gift,
Single heart to heaven lift;
Here remain if thou wouldst be
Palmer in all verity:
Know thy faith doth brighter shine
Than the lamps within the shrine.

(39)

FIGHTING THE WIND.

The Psylli border on the Nasamonians; these perished in the
following manner: the south wind blowing upon them dried up
all their water-tanks, and the whole country within Syrtis was
dry; they, therefore, having consulted together, with one con-
sent determined to make war against that wind (I only repeat
what the Libyans say), and when they arrived at the sands the
south wind, blowing, covered them over, and when they had
perished the Nasamonians took possession of their territory. —
HERODOTUS, iv. 173.

HEAR what befell a dusk race that dwelt in a Libyan
    land,
Between the desert-like sea and the wandering sea-like
    sand !

Steadily blew the south wind, cloudless the days filed
    by,
Till void were the oasis wells, their chambers crannied
    and dry.
Fell the lank fruit unripened, — so fiercely the siroc
    burned ;
The blade returned to the earth, and the foodless
    cattle returned.

Light was the brain of the people, goaded by hunger
    and thirst ;

The beckoning palms and the fountain that mocked in
  the looming they cursed.
Black were their fever-burnt lips, and starting their
  feverish eyes,
Like wailful voices of autumn their hollow, delirious
  cries.
"Let us," they said, "bear arms, go forth, and make
  war on our foe,
The Wind that is sent from the South by the God who
  worketh our woe!"

Then they arose in their madness, and clad them in
  battle array,
Stripped from the savage wild beasts that seek in the
  mountains their prey;
Skins of the pard and the lion, and mane-waving hel-
  mets they wore,
And many an amulet trusted in fight at their girdles
  they bore.

Then seize they the bow and the arrows more poison
  than fang of the asp;
Lift they the spear and the leathern shield in their
  tremulous grasp;
Beat they on drums, and through shells of the ocean
  faintly they blow,
Faintly the war-cry sound, advancing to close with
  their foe. . . .

Him and his legions they saw not, appareled in darkness and heat;

They heard but his chariot wheels, the thunder of on-
coming feet.
But once their keen arrows they winged, but once
their javelins drove :
Then stricken they lay in the dust ; under dust no
longer they strove!
For, as seas are heaped up by the storm in its fury and
might,
So rose the great surge of the desert and hid them forever from sight.

Thou hearest the tale as it runs in the chronicle faded
and old :
Canst thou read it anew and aright?   Of thee, Human
Heart, it is told !
Look! thou art parched and hungered ; look how thou
armest in vain
To fight the invincible Wind, — to be laid in the dust
of the plain !

A NOCTURN.

I HAVE been an acolyte
In the service of the Night;
Subtile incense I have burned,
Songs of silence I have learned, —
Spirit-uttered antiphon
That from isle to isle doth run
Through the deep cathedral wood.
There she blessed me as I stood, —
There, or in her courts that lie
Open to the gemmèd sky.
Me with starlight she hath crowned,
And with purple wrapped me round, —
Darkling purple, strangely wrought
By the servants of her thought.

Mortal, whosoe'er thou art,
That dost bear a fevered heart,
Hither come and healèd be :
Night such grace will show to thee,
Thou shalt tread the dewy stubble
Stranger to all fret and trouble,
While bright Hesper leans from heaven
Through the soft, dove-colored even,

(43)

A NOCTURN.

While the grass-bird calleth peace
On the fields that have release
From the sickle and the rake.
Happy sigher! thou shalt take
The rich breath of blossomed maize,
As the moist wind smoothly plays
With its misty silks and plumes.
Thou shalt peer through tangled glooms,
Where the fruited brier-rose
Fragrance on thy pathway throws,
And the firefly bears a link ;
Where swart bramble-berries drink
Spicy dew, and shall be sweet,
Ripened by to-morrow's heat:
Still, wherever thou dost pass,
Chimes the cricket in the grass ;
And the plover's note is heard, —
Moonlight's wild enchanted bird,
Flitting, wakeful and forlorn,
Round the meadows lately shorn.

Wilt thou come, and healèd be
Of the wounds Day gave to thee ? —
Come and dwell, an acolyte
Of the deep-browed holy Night.

THE SURPRISE.

Joy met Sorrow in a place
Where the branches interlace,
Very secret, still, and sweet,
Safe from all profaning feet.
" Why art here ? " Joy, startled, cried ;
" Why art here ? " gray Sorrow sighed.

" I came here to weep," said Joy.
" Tears are ever my employ,"
    Murmured Sorrow.   " Yet I see
Tears as grateful were to thee.
Come, young novice, and be taught
How to ease thy heart o'erfraught."

Joy sat down at Sorrow's feet,
And was taught a lesson sweet.
Fain would he make kind return :
"Sorrow, art too old to learn?
Nay ?   Then tarry yet a while,
Till I 've taught thee how to smile ! "

Since that hour the two have been
Bound as by mysterious kin ;

Since that hour they so exchange
Tears and smiles, 't is nothing strange
If sometimes a puzzled heart
Scarce can tell the twain apart.

A HUMMING-BIRD.

Somewhere I've seen thee, strange sprite,
   Somewhere I've known thee ere now,
Among the wild broods of the night
   That nest on the Morphean bough!

Thou with a silent throat
   Dost busily rifle all blooms;
O flitter-winged bandit, thy note
   Is the bee's song shed from thy plumes!

Whisper those things in my ear,
   That thou art so ready to tell
To creatures too heedless to hear, —
   The lily, the foxglove's bell!

Aha! is it so? — By these eyes,
   Prospero's servant I see, —
Ariel clad in the guise
   Of a humming-bird lightsome and free!

(47)

THE WRECKER.

Out, out, ye gnashing, hungry pack,
  And scour the desert salt and wide !
But what ye take bring straightway back,
  And toss it hither up the tide.

From main to main ye coursing go,
  Ye bring the deep-hulled ships to bay ;
And then returned with sure reflow,
  Your captures on the beach ye lay.

Is it Iberian grapes ye bring,
  Or slender length of Indian cane ?
Or is it some old sovereign's ring
  That long in secret gulfs hath lain ?

Ye will not bring me these to-day ?
  Then cast me here upon the shore
A mast the storm hath shorn away,
  A rudder, or a broken oar.

I build my boat, — a fisher's smack ;
  I build it well, ye seamen gone,
With what the waves have yielded back,
  The timbers from your vessels drawn.

I build my house on seaboard ground,
  I build it well with far-brought trees ;
With blanchèd drift made smooth and round
  By the swift lathe of circling seas.

To whom should I a salvage pay ?
  To you who drank the mortal deep,
Whose craving hands reach through the spray,
  Whose voices sound within my sleep !

WOODCRAFT.

He makes his way with speed and ease
Through woods that show the noonday star;
The moss-grown trunks of oldest trees
    His lettered guide-boards are.

The tameless bee he follows home;
He marks in air the path it beats,
The hollow oak that holds the comb,
    With all its trickling sweets.

The gnarly vine no vintner binds,
To him swings down its purple hoard;
The shade-embosomed spring he finds,
    His drinking-cup a gourd.

Lacks he a roof? — the withe he bends,
The bough he pleaches overhead;
A couch? — the fallen leafage lends
    A soft and fragrant bed.

Lacks he a fire? — the kindling spark
He bids the chafèd wood reveal;
Lacks he a boat? — of birchen bark
    He frames a lightsome keel.

And that he may not savage be,
He carves a flute whose yearning tones,
Upon a summer eve set free,
    Wake love in clods and stones.

A FLUTE.

" How shall I liken thee, reed of my choice,
Spirit-like, fugitive, wavering voice ? "

" I am an oread lost to the hills,
Sick for the mountain wind tossing my rills;
Sighing from memory snatches of song
Pine-trees have sung to me all the night long;
Shrouded they sang to me, mingling my dreams;
Down through their tapestries planets shot gleams.
Eagles on cliffs between heaven and me
Looked from their watch-towers, far on the sea."

" How wast thou taken, sweet, — lost to the hills,
Footprints of thine no more seen by the rills ? "

" Quickly I answer thee : Sorrow came by,
Made me her foster-child, loving my cry ! "

(52)

THE WILD SOWER.

UP and down the land I go,
　　Through the valley, over hill ;
Many a pleasant ground I sow,
　　Never one I reap or till ;
Fan and flail I never wield,
Leave no hayrick in the field.

Farmer goes with leathern scrip,
　　Fills the harrowed earth with seed ;
In the selfsame score I slip
　　Germs of many a lusty weed.
Though I scatter in his track,
I possess nor bin nor sack.

He sows wheat, and I sow tare,
　　Rain and sunshine second toil ;
Tame and wild these acres share,
　　Wrestling for the right of soil.
I stand by and clap my hands,
Cheering on my urchin bands.

Mine the cockle in the rye,
　　Thronèd thistle, large and fine,

And the daisy's white-fringed eye,
   And the dodder's endless twine;
Mine those fingers five that bind
Every blade and stalk they find.

Mine the lilies, hot and bright,
   Setting summer meads on fire;
Mine the silkweed's spindles white,
   Spinning Autumn's soft attire.
Golden-rod and aster then
I bring up by bank and glen.

Whoso fleeth to the woods,
   Whoso buildeth on the plains,
I, too, seek those solitudes,
   Leading on my hardy trains:
Thorn and brier, still man's lot,
Crowd around the frontier cot.

Many serve me, unaware, —
   Shaggy herds that ceaseless roam,
And the rovers of the air
   Passing to their winter home;
More than these upon me wait, —
Wind and water bear my freight.

Thus, a sower wild, I go,
   Trafficking with every clime;
Still the fruitful germs I sow
   That shall vex your harvest-time;
Otherwise, ye toil-stooped men,
Eden's ease were come again!

THE SPHINX.

In these fields there lives a sphinx :
Woe to him who rashly thinks
He hath wit to overreach
What her servants cannot teach !

Thou shalt never see her face,
Yet her presence fills the place ;
Thou shalt never meet her eyes,
Yet their light, reflected, lies
On the polished streams that flow,
And on flowers that catch the glow.
Thou shalt never hear her voice,
Yet it is her sov'reign choice
That the winds should breathe her will
Unto grove, and vale, and hill ;
That the hills should answer back
Storms that drive the cloudy rack
On its lightning-cloven track ;
That the morning should not lack
Sweet antheming, nor evening be
Without its mellow minstrelsy.

Dost thou boast that thou canst **read**
The easy legend of a mead ?

Then the grass doth bid thee show,
In an hour, how much 't will grow,
How so soon it can repair
Plots the sheep have nibbled bare.
Hast thou peered beneath the hoods
Of the genii of the woods?
Canst thou, passing by their cells,
Understand their muttered spells?
Canst thou read their curious work
Traced on scrolls of hoary birk?
Wilt thou try to count the mast
That the acorn-trees have cast?
Or tell what needle, deft and fine,
Stitched the broad leaves of the vine?
Honey bees, with sacs of sweet,
Plundering every flower they meet,
Bid thee say what part goes home,
Nectar pure or cellèd comb.
The building bird, with straw or shred,
Holds askance her cunning head,
Tries thy wisdom by her test, —
Canst thou build or weave a nest?
When thou makest no reply,
Round the fields soft laughters fly,
And the rumor goes abroad
That this man, or demi-god,
Reaching for the Infinite,
Cannot, with his best of wit,
Solve what hath for ages lain
An open secret, fair and plain!

A CHILD OF EARTH.

Ye meadows and maize-waving fields,
Warm orchards, with your mellow yields,
And fallows, joyous and unkempt;
Ye woodlands, whether gray or green,
As Spring in you doth sleep or wake;
Ye trivial runs, that ever tempt
The longest way to reach your home,
And, as ye wander, ever break
Green news to banks ye glide between;
Thou quiet shore, and thou serene,
Cool under-heaven, dashed with foam
(Wide water, glad in thy approach), —
O ye, my kindred! hear me now,
While I my love and service broach;
Your claim I may not disallow.

I am of thee, thou patient soil;
Thy harvests here, that bend and bow,
And make long pathways for the breeze;
Thine ancient clansmen, strong with toil
(Thine old storm-proven growths, the trees);
Thy fondlings recent from the germ,
Which dew and beam make haste to find, —
All cognate are to me, and kind!

I am of these, and taught by these
To strike my roots down deep and firm.

Ye veering streams, where'er ye ply,
I seek you with a thirsty mind:
In summer, when ye climb the sky,
And leave your channels cracked and dry,
Burns fever in my dwindled veins;
And when in your white cells ye lie,
And soundless hammers forge your chains,
My fluid thought is bound with gyves,
And mute and dull as ye remains.
Wide water, with thy Protean lives,
In counting of thy tribute gains,
Miss not the streams that draw to thee
From sources in the heart of me.

My kindred! forest, field, and lake!
Once more I right confession make
How dear to me ye ever were,
And, while I live by breath, shall be:
When breath is past, 't is yours to take,
Mournless, the never wanderer,
And gently, without sound or stir,
His elements among you break, —
Whose heaven shall perchance be fair
With types of you, immortal there.

SWEET CIDER.

Soul of the apple glorified!
In a sudden flush of pride,
I would send this blameless beaker
To that mellow pleasure-seeker,
Old Anacreon, with this boast:
"Take some joy on Pluto's coast;
Here's a drink with more sunshine
Than e'er laughed in Levant wine!"

(59)

ST. JOHN'S EVE.

"We have the receipt of fern-seed, — we walk invisible."

UPON St. John's Eve they who wear
    The seed of crafty fern,
Where'er they list abroad may fare,
    And none shall them discern.

On yester-eve the charm I tried ;
    The magic seed I brought
From secret glen, though long defied,
    By elf and pixy fought.

    .   .   .   .   .   .

None gave good-even as I passed,
    None bent a look on me ;
I sought the linden path and, last,
    The broad, green trysting-tree.

My lady there I thought to meet,
    And yet unseen remain,
To read her face in silence sweet,
    And deeper heart-lore gain.

I nothing saw, — nor glimmering robe,
    Nor white hand part the boughs ;
The poisèd blowball's feathery globe
    There was no wind to rouse ;

(60)

Yet oft the grass was stirred, and oft
    The flower on nodding stem,
As pressed by footstep light and soft,
    Or brushed by floating hem.

" He will not come, — he loves not me,"
    A voice sighed 'midst the dew ;
Though I nor face nor form could see,
    Full well the voice I knew.

" He will not come, — he loves me not,"
    More near the murmur drew ;
Aha ! my lady has her plot,
    She wears the fern-seed too !

" But I am here," I answer brought,
    " That may'st thou know by this" —
Her viewless hand by chance I caught,
    And on it pressed a kiss.

"Trust not to charms, my wizard queen,
    But heed a wizard's word :
We on St. John's Eve walk unseen,
    Not (saints forbid !) unheard ! "

THE NIGHT IS STILL.

THE night is still, the moon looks kind,
    The dew hangs jewels in the heath,
An ivy climbs across thy blind,
    And throws a light and misty wreath.

The dew hangs jewels in the heath,
    Buds bloom for which the bee has pined;
I haste along, I quicker breathe,
    The night is still, the moon looks kind.

Buds bloom for which the bee has pined,
    The primrose slips its jealous sheath,
As up the flower-watched path I wind
    And come thy window-ledge beneath.

The primrose slips its jealous sheath, —
    Then open wide that churlish blind,
And kiss me through the ivy wreath!
    The night is still, the moon looks kind.

(62)

TO THE EVENING STAR.

LIFT thy face of silver daybreak through the dusky
  evening sky,
Regent of the emptied heavens when the sun-god stoops
  to die!
   By the glimmer of thine eye
Well I know thou art that Hesper who in distant twi-
  light time,
Wandering on great hills of Afric, watched the con-
  stellations climb
   To the noon of nights sublime;
Brother of the giant Atlas, who in desert plains of earth
Heaved his mighty shoulder, bracing up the heavens'
  hollow girth,
   When the worlds were fresh from birth!

Age by age thou didst keep vigil, wrapped in folds of
  wizard blue,
Tracing on a parchment forms of beauty prime creation
  knew,
   Till thy shape a shadow grew,
Till the blest Immortals drew thee, reaching down
  empyreal space,
Lit thy brows, and bade thee forward on the planets'
  orbic race!
   By the daybreak in thy face,

Art thou not, O wise Enchanter, now become Love's
    leading star ?
Wouldst thou not provide a pilot, if in wingèd ship or
    car
        He should near thy harbor-bar ?

Hast thou not for him a mansion based in purple fields
    of air,
Set with many a crystal window opening on a vistaed
    stair, —
        Velvet inner chambers rare ?
Hast thou not for him a garden, with a river flowing
    round,
Where the apple-flower is cradled, slopes with vine and
    olive crowned,
        Groves that breathe a minstrel sound ?

Are not all the brave and lovely, whose smooth voices
    fill the wind,
While a sweet and flying murmur haunts us whom they
    leave behind,
        Gone to thee by pathway blind ?
Do they rest in flower-sown meadows, or beneath the
    forest side ?
Do they gaze between the columns of thy fretted
    porches wide,
        On the ebb of sunset tide ?
Trembles now thy blissful planet with their laughter and
    their song,
Till the farthest stars are kindled and the wistful shin-
    ing throng
        To thy music moves along ?

THE STRANGE GUEST.

HE brought a branch of olive —
   This stranger guest of mine;
Could I deny him entrance,
   Who bore the peaceful sign?
Ah no! I bade him welcome,
   I set him meat and wine;
But while he drank and feasted,
   How laughed his eyes divine!

I took the branch of olive
   (The soothest plant that grows),
And from the carven ceiling
   I hung it with the rose.
" But why to me this token,
   Who never lacked repose?
Why this to me," I questioned,
   " Who know nor feud nor foes? "

He smiled beneath the olive —
   This strangest stranger guest.
A branch from off the thorn-tree
   Had told his errand best;
For since my house he entered
   There 's ne'er a heart at rest.
To mock me with the olive!
   But Love doth love his jest.

(65)

" FOR THE TIME BEING."

"For the time being!"
How long is that?   A space as brief
As takes the whirling autumn leaf
To reach the sward, the April flake
To change to dew, the wave to break,
    Now shoreward fleeing?

"For the time being!"
How long is that?   As long, perchance,
As while a merry thought doth glance
Across the deep of well-loved eyes?
As long as term of tears and sighs,
    The full heart freeing?

"For the time being!"
How long is that?   (I wait to hear.)
A breathing space, a day, a year?
Till this life's silent bound be won
And other unknown life begun,
    Past sound, past seeing?

"For the time being!"
It is forever, as I think,
A ceaseless adding link to link,

A series, as of waves at sea ;
For, tell me, when shall time not be,
     In Fate's decreeing?

     " For the time being ! "
It is thy word.   Thou dost not know
Such promise will not let thee go ;
Since time shall never cease to be,
I ask but this, — that thou 'lt love me
     " For the time being ! "

SOLSTICE.

In the month of June, when the world is green,
When the dew beads thick on the clover spray,
And the noons are rife with the scent of hay,
And the brook hides under a willow screen ;
When the rose is queen, in Love's demesne,
Then, the time is too sweet and too light to stay :
Whatever the sun and the dial say,
      This is the shortest day !

In the month of December, when, naked and keen,
The tree-tops thrust at the snow-cloud gray,
And frozen tears fill the lids of day ;
When only the thorn of the rose is seen,
Then, in heavy teen, each breath between,
We sigh, " Would the winter were well away ! "
Whatever the sun and the dial say,
      This is the longest day !

IN TRUST.

Love itself cannot bestow,
Heaven bestowed Love long ago.
Sweet the error of thy thought,
If it deem I give thee aught,
Who but render back thine own,
Destined thine from time unknown.
Gladly it reverts to thee,
Casting off my regency:
So the carrier-dove, when freed,
Cannot choose but homeward speed;
So the flower-lent dewdrop flies
Back unto its native skies;
So the brightness of the wave
But returns what Titan gave;
So the voice from out the hill
Runneth at the bidder's will;
So the soul that hidden lies
In the flute, now lives, now dies,
Mastered by a breath and touch.
Only this I marvel much:
Heaven, designing gifts for thee,
Placed them here in trust with me.

(69)

A BIRTHDAY GREETING.

TO J. L. T.

AH, fair in age! if thou hadst lived in Greece,
  At wise Athena's feast thou hadst been named
To bear aloft the olive of pure peace,
  With those in winter years for graces famed.

(70)

MUSA VICTRIX.

WHO can bar the way of song?
Who can do the Muse a wrong?
Ne'er could bondsman bondsman be,
If she willed to set him free.
Though he kept Admetus' flocks,
He would see the trees and rocks,
And a thousand wild feet dancing
To his pipes and glees entrancing!

Thoroughfares and crowded courts
Cannot spoil the Muse's sports;
Walls scholastic, tradesman's frown,
Cannot hedge nor put her down:
While we plod, she 's flown to find
Haunts more suited to her mind;
Or, if any should gainsay,
She can sweep the crowd away,
Bound and landmark can displace
For her royal pleasure-chase.

Oh, the masker! Oh, the scout!
Deft as Love, in seeking out
Those on whom she casts her charm!
Once upon a mountain farm,

As a plowman drove the share,
Fell a blossom small and fair;
Then she bade him sing for pity
The shorn daisy's passing ditty.
Once into a lecture-room,
On a morn of summer bloom,
Phœbus sent an arrow bright;
Only one with eyes of light
Did divine that airy flame:
" Through the room a sunbeam came,
Troops of shining creatures in it!
No delay — that very minute
I was off, with their light band,
To Oberon and Fairyland!"

Who can bar the way of song?
Who can do the Muse a wrong?
Sooner may the streams be reined,
Or the noonday sunbeams chained!

SONG AND SILENCE.

LONELY art thou in thy sorrow — lonely art thou;
Yet, lone as thou art, at least it is left thee to sing:
Thy heart-blood staining the thorn on the secret bough,
    Make the deep woodland ring!

Well-friended art thou in thy joy — well-friended art
    thou;
No longer, Love-kept as thou art, it is left thee to sing:
Thou, in thy down-soft nest on the summer bough,
    Foldest both song and wing.

(73)

BETWEEN TWO SEASONS.

Summer 's lingering, homesick bird,
Winter's tree the frost hath furred,
Summer's grass-blade starting light
Through the Winter's mantle white;
Summer's flower and Winter's flake,
Grievous sight!
(Down, poor Summer, else my heart will break!)

Youth, a shepherd piping blithe;
Age, a caitiff with a scythe;
Youth, warm faith and eager gust;
Age, chill cavil and distrust;
Youth the dreamer, Age awake, —
Part ye must!
(Down, poor Youth, or else my heart will break!)

(74)

THE CHRISTMAS ANGEL.

DEAREST, I never lacked from thee a gift,
  Nor thou from me, until this Christmas-tide,
  When more than Summer's wreckèd treasures hide
Beneath the stainless, smooth, wind-sculptured drift.

What largess once love's least bestowal brought !
  But change has come since thou art wandered hence ;
  How can I reach thee in thy affluence ?
Can Earth bestow when Heaven requireth naught ?

All blessedness is thine, — thou still canst give,
  I but receive ; and since this must suffice,
  Entreat thou of our Lord in Paradise,
For me, the gift of patience while I live.

And come thou when the red dawn-fire is blown,
  And rocking fir-trees shed the snow's light fleece ;
  Come with the Christmas angels, singing peace, —
They to the wide world, thou to me alone !

ANGEL CHORUS.

Be peace on earth !   Clear peace,
That hath its springs in love,

(75)

Descend, and flow through earth
   As through the courts above ;
Let restless mortals feel
   The broodings of the Dove.
As night-winds lapse at dawn,
   As calms the oilèd wave,
Let anger fail of breath,
   And hatred find its grave ;
For Heaven still waits to give
   As Heaven in old-time gave.

A VOICE ALONE.

Peace in thy heart! Pure peace,
   My sorrowing love, be thine !
Thy night was deep and dark,
   But daybreak brings a sign, —
Amid the angels' song
   God lets thee hearken mine.
Thy own in years of time,
   Lo, I am still thy own
Where time no measure knows,
   Before our Maker's throne ;
I am not reft of thee,
   Nor bidest thou alone.

ANGEL CHORUS.

Good-will on earth! Good-will
   Among well-pleasured men,
Who carve the ways whereby
   Their King shall come again, —

Who carve and wait, nor ask
   How He shall come, or when.
The rose shall then spring up,
   To conquer waste and wild,
And might and frailty be
   Forever reconciled;
The lion and the lamb
   Be guided by a child!

A VOICE ALONE.

Good-will be in thy heart,
   To all who thee surround!
Bear balm to others' hurt
   And this shall close thy wound;
So thou on earth and I
   In heaven be closer bound.
For all my life is love,
   And love thy life should be;
Oh, let love's shadow, grief,
   Divide not thee and me;
Look where the dawn-rose blooms,
   And there my signal see.

MONITORS.

THE pure heart looked upon the midnight skies, —
"God's pity for the soul who feels the eyes
  Of all these heavenly censors flash reproof
  For sin that keepeth him from Thee aloof!"

The foul heart looked upon the midnight skies,
But there might see nor heavenly censors' eyes,
  Nor feel their holy check upon his ways,
  Though he all night till morning-tide should gaze.

Behold! guilt's hardihood this guerdon earns, —
Silent the monitors where'er it turns!
  And therefore pray, pure heart, God's pity be
  On him whom dulling sin forbids to see.

(78)

THE QUIET PILGRIM.

What shall I say? He hath both spoken unto me, and Himself hath done it: I shall go softly all my years in the bitterness
of my soul. — ISAIAH xxxviii. 15.

WHEN on my soul in nakedness
His swift, avertless hand did press,
Then I stood still, nor cried aloud,
Nor murmured low in ashes bowed;
And, since my woe is utterless,
To supreme quiet I am vowed;
Afar from me be moan and tears, —
I shall go softly all my years.

Whenso my quick, light-sandaled feet
Bring me where Joys and Pleasures meet,
I mingle with their throng at will;
They know me not an alien still,
Since neither words nor ways unsweet
Of storèd bitterness I spill;
Youth shuns me not, nor gladness fears, —
For I go softly all my years.

Whenso I come where Griefs convene,
And in my ear their voice is keen,

They know me not, as on I glide,
That with Arch Sorrow I abide.
They haggard are, and drooped of mien,
And round their brows have cypress tied :
Such shows I leave to light Grief's peers, —
I shall go softly all my years.

Yea, softly ! heart of hearts unknown.
Silence hath speech that passeth moan,
More piercing-keen than breathèd cries
To such as heed, make sorrow-wise.
But save this voice without a tone,
That runs before me to the skies,
And rings above thy ringing spheres,
Lord, I go softly all my years !

THE OTHER FACE OF NIGHT.

I SORROWED, slept; and this my dream:
I looked, and saw large Hesper gleam
Right in the east, above the bar
Of morning mists, — a morning star.
Full-lustred, tremulous, he stood,
Throbbing on silent stream and wood.
"Behold!" I cried, " that watcher bright,
Who trims the lamp of jealous Night,
Hath on a stolen errand gone,
To do the service of the Dawn."

Then spake a voice, serene in air:
"Thou art new-come, nor yet aware
How the calm heavens of the dead
Above thee and around are spread;
So marvelest thou that Hesper clear
Doth in the van of Dawn appear.
But from thy brow chase vexing thought,
And be thou apt, and soothly taught:
The star of eve to sorrowing men
Is morning star in spirits' ken.
Thou seest the other face of Night,
And planets flushed with Orient light."

I dreamed, and woke, and did rejoice,
So dwelt with me the blessèd voice.

WHAT WORD?

Out of the West what word,
What word out of the West?
    (O voiceful wind!)
Say — and thy flight be blest —
Say if the elfin bird
Still pours from its nest in the breast of my Best
  Flute-note and caroled song,
    All the day long!

Out of the West this word,
This word out of the West:
    (O lover blind!)
Sorrow, a sullen guest,
Hath hunted the elfin bird
Out of its nest in the breast of thy Best;
  Silence there, and no song
    All the day long!
        (82)

THE PASSING OF THE LETTERS.

THE mail from the east and the mail from the west —
　A thunder of wheels — a rushing blast!
The drowsy travelers never guessed
　What voices arose as the two trains passed.

" Tell him you met me, tell him I fly! "
　" That will I!　Tell her I stay not nor rest! "
Thus greeted Love's messengers speeding by,
　One from the east and one from the west.

MOLY.

> The root is hard to loose
> From hold of earth by mortals; but Gods' power
> Can all things do.   'T is black, but bears a flower
> As white as milk.   (CHAPMAN'S *Homer.*)

TRAVELER, pluck a stem of moly,
  If thou touch at Circe's isle, —
Hermes' moly, growing solely
  To undo enchanter's wile!
When she proffers thee her chalice, —
Wine and spices mixed with malice, —
When she smites thee with her staff
To transform thee, do thou laugh!
Safe thou art if thou but bear
The least leaf of moly rare.
Close it grows beside her portal,
Springing from a stock immortal, —
Yes! and often has the Witch
Sought to tear it from its niche;
But to thwart her cruel will
The wise God renews it still.
Though it grows in soil perverse,
Heaven hath been its jealous nurse,
And a flower of snowy mark
Springs from root and sheathing dark;

Kingly safeguard, only herb
That can brutish passion curb !
Some do think its name should be
Shield-Heart, White Integrity.
Traveler, pluck a stem of moly,
    If thou touch at Circe's isle, —
Hermes' moly, growing solely
    To undo enchanter's wile !

HUMILITY.

I PLUCKED the weeds forth, left and right,
    To make an open space
About a wind-sown blossom bright,
    With uplift wondering face.

" Why sparest me, and them dost slay ? "
    The darling blossom sighed ;
Nor knew itself more worth than they
    That fell in rank-blown pride.

LIBERTY.

How winneth Liberty?   By sword and brand,
　Or by the souls of those who strive and die?
Where dwelleth Liberty?   Where lies the land
　Most open to the favors of her eye?
Hath she her seat in empires, deserts wide,
Or most in little freeholds doth she bide?

What is the range that Nature gives her own?
　With frost or fire she stays their flying feet,
And holdeth each within its native zone:
　The pine its love — the palm, shall never meet;
Nowhere do roses bloom from beds of ice,
Nowhere in valleys laughs the edelweiss.

The races of the sea shall never fare
　Beyond the moist and sounding element,
Nor any pinion, fledged and schooled in air,
　On venturous errand through the waves be sent:
The cygnet to his nest of river flag,
The eagle to his aerie on the crag.

Dwells Freedom with the sphery multitude
　The vistas of the nightly sky reveal?

Each planet keeps the track it hath pursued,
  And shall pursue while ages turn and wheel;
Uncentred, roves the guideless aerolite,
And drives to ruin down the steeps of night.

With law dwells liberty; law maketh free;
  Fly law, and thou dost forge thyself a chain.
Still wouldst thou pass the limits set for thee?
  Still wouldst thou grasp strange honors and domain?
Behold, his liberty exceedeth thine,
Who freely breathes in bounds where thou wouldst
    pine!

THE CUP.

Thou that didst fashion forth this chalice frail
By marvelous and secret workmanship,
Whate'er the potion lifted to my lip,
    Let not my spirit fail.

So temper Thou for me joy's lusty wine,
That no presumptuous madness it shall breed;
And cast Thou into praise's subtle mead
    An amethyst divine.

In that dull stream which runs from sorrow's press,
Mingle a keen elixir, lest my powers,
Fallen on silent and oblivious hours,
    Should lapse in idleness.

Do thou allay remorse's fiery heat,
Blending therewith a blessed lenitive,
So that I wither not away, but live
    To make amendment meet.

Teach me a golden song, that worthily
Life's affluent vintage I may celebrate;
And put into my heart a pledge elate
    For them that drink with me.

Thou that didst fashion forth this fragile cup,
Upon that day when Thou shalt pour therein
The draught that must dissolve its substance thin,
Lift Thou my spirit up!

RETRIEVAL.

An inward counselor gave me this behest :
" Throw from thee what thou hast, and take a quest ;
Go forth a beggar, and with sweet address
      Make suit for Happiness."

The fervent voice I hastened to obey.
That which I had in hand I threw away,
Nor gave it thought, so longed I to possess
      Far-dwelling Happiness.

I went a beggar meek, with craving hand ;
The bosom-prompter cried, " Demand ! demand ! "
Some laughed, some chid, to see how I did press
      My suit for Happiness.

. . . .

When life ran low and dear daylight grew late,
I turned me home ; at my neglected gate
A palmer stood. "He waits (methought) to bless
      With long-sought Happiness."

The palmer smiled — through tears he smiled on me :
" Not so, fond beggar ; I but save to thee
What thou didst cast away, — nor more, nor less, —
      Thy Peace, not Happiness."

(91)

THE LEADER.

HAIL to the leaders of men, the sovereigns by grace of
    God,
Who flinch not and fear not to venture where none be-
    fore them have trod !
As lightning unsheathed from the clouds to chasten the
    pestilent air,
As fire running swift through the sere-wood, their spirit
    shall Heaven prepare.

Lo, the armed leader alone ! But soon not single he
    stands ;
Not quicker sown teeth of the dragon sprang up in
    militant bands
About the great founder of Thebes than rallying le-
    gions arise,
And circle a leader of men, and lift his loved name to
    the skies.
Then, whereso he biddeth them strike, there draw they
    the glittering blade,
And whereso he biddeth them pause, the tide of the
    battle is stayed ;
The field being won, he teacheth how victors should
    temper their pride ;

The field being lost, how Truth and the Right beyond
    ravage abide.
Few are the leaders of men, yet many the liegemen
    they draw;
Fire of the courage in one, chill fear in a thousand shall
    thaw!
Still, as of old, Miltiades' trophies drive away sleep,
Still at the parle of the trumpet hearts responsive shall
    leap:
Wherefore we follow our leaders, and well! yet cannot
    discern
How they whom we follow exultant are also led in their
    turn.
But surely, unseen is their chieftain, no plume stream-
    ing white in their van, —
Ah, surely, unseen is their chieftain, and ever a greater
    than man!
We move as their watchword commands; but a watch-
    word more potent they hear:
The clang of the battle for us, for them music aerial-
    clear!
(So he who drank poison at Athens still heard the
    sweet voice of the law,
As the wild Corybantes the flutes of their deity listened
    in awe.)

They follow a deathless Idea, — leader of leaders for
    aye,
That liveth, and wageth its strife, though we remain
    but a day;
That chooseth the man most fit, and setteth him fore-
    most in fray:

Hail to the leaders of men, who know and their leader
    obey!
Yet we too, the liegemen, — we too, though our sight
    exceed not a span, —
Follow a deathless Idea clothed in a puissant man.

APOLLO THE SHEPHERD.

An exile since the summer's reign was new,
  All day I range the broad, path-checkered land,
And sleep at night beneath the moon and dew,
  A shepherd's staff and scrip laid close at hand.
Low seems my state, a lowly hireling's guise,
    Yet am I richly served as any king
      Whose palace walls are stretched for many a rood.
My palace walls are merged in bending skies;
    My servitors haste every way, and bring
      Cool amber honey from the hollow wood,
    And in my cup the vintage clusters wring.
      They flit before me in the solitude,
Their kind eyes smiling through their glistening locks;
Love greets me here, though keeper of Admetus' flocks.

So well the god I mask, they know me not, —
    Young shepherds of the hills, who gather round,
Care-loosed at evening, or in noontides hot
    Stretched in the shadow on some chosen ground;
They know me not, who feed upon my songs
    And flute-blown memories of the golden lyre,
      Once heard upon Olympus' mansioned height,
Where the smooth pavement glassed the leaning throngs

That listened breathless, all their hearts on fire,
  In the deep, starlit, nectar-flowing night !
Men know me not, yet I the wilds inspire ;
  Glad beasts draw near, and birds in circling flight,
While voices waken in the mountain rocks,
And hail me king, though keeper of Admetus' flocks.

Where go ye now astray, ye zealous bards,
  And sigh your spirits forth for love of me ?
Leave now the drowsy groves, the garden swards,
  The myrtle bowers, where ye are wont to be ;
No longer seek for me at Delphi's shrine,
  Nor where steep Helicon his freshness spills,
  Nor at my island home amidst the seas,
Nor yet with flowers my templed image twine :
  Come up to me, among the heathy hills,
  Led by the whispering of laurel-trees,
The conscious echoes and the muse-taught rills ;
  Listen, and trace my deity by these ;
It is my hand the source of song unlocks, —
I am your king, come keep with me Admetus' flocks !

THE HOMESICKNESS OF GANYMEDE.

EAGLE pinions, swift as thought,
Ganymede to heaven brought,
Stolen from the plains of Troy,
Loved of gods, immortal boy!
Still a stranger in the skies,
Ganymede in heaven sighs.

In Jove's palace full of light
He doth serve the nectar bright;
Smile on him the Ever-Blest,
As he moves to do their hest:
Downward still he bends his eyes, —
Still a stranger in the skies!

When each godhead, drinking deep,
Sinks beneath the tide of sleep,
Ganymede on wingèd feet
Hastes where sky and mountain meet:
Soft the mist around him lies,
Ganymede in heaven sighs.

River, field, and wooded height
Swim together in his sight;

He can only guess how fair,
In the moonlit, midnight air,
Ilion's walls and turrets rise, —
Still a stranger in the skies !

He can only dream how sweet
Are the ways where mortals meet, —
Chariot-race, or hunter's spear,
Temple service, vintage cheer,
Young maid's laughter, youth's fond eyes :
Ganymede in heaven sighs !

Haply men have seen him gaze
Through the summer-evening haze,
Leaning past the piny crest
Of the mountain in the west,
Wavering there in star-bright guise,
Still a stranger in the skies !

Careless gods, take back your gift,
Or his human heart uplift :
Deathless youth ye gave in sport,
Deathless sorrow haunts your court.
Still a stranger in the skies,
Ganymede in heaven sighs.

THE KINGFISHER.

"While birds of calm sit brooding on the charmèd wave."

THE north is flocking with snow, with plumes that were
    fledged in the sky;
The east is a garden of thorns where the frost's keen
    javelins fly;
The west is a world of caverns whence storms are un-
    leashed for the chase, —
Alcyone, tarry we here in the sun of the south for a
    space!
Rest, for the air is softer than dreams that hover in
    sleep;
Rest, for the summer rests with us, mantling the gulf
    and the steep.
The long-severed rivers are folded at last in the arms
    of the sea,
With drift from the thyme-sweet meadows, and sheaves
    they have caught from the lea.
The riotous winds and the ocean are bound by a truce
    for thy sake,
And well may the mariner sing, for he knows that no
    flaw will awake, —
Thou flying in languorous curves or dipping thy breast
    in the spray.

Now I will call to thee, dearest, from cliffs that o'er-
  shadow the bay,
And tell thee what thou didst forego when a god gave
  thee right of the air,
Sped thee on wings and sent thee, a herald of seasons
  most fair !

Far hence is the land of our sires, that laughs with
  green fields all the year:
There shepherds are hardy, and foresters light with the
  bow and the spear ;
Harvestmen reap and bind, slow breasting the golden-
  ripe flood ;
Youth chants the burden for Linus, when presses are
  shedding his blood.
I was the king of all these, and a prince in the battles
  of men ;
The day-star of empire that set in my fall arose not
  again.
In the night, and afar from all coasts where a beacon
  gives joy to the crew,
The break-faith sea and the sharp-fanged rocks that are
  hidden from view
Close on their prey with hoarse bayings, — there reft
  were mine eyes of the light,
But thy name, Alcyone, flew from my lips, with the
  breath taking flight !

Long didst thou sit in the haven, awaiting the dawn of
  my fleet,
Imploring the sea and the spirits that track it with
  murmurous feet,

And oft wouldst thou question the traders that came
    with the purples of Tyre :
A god raised thee up, when thou leap'dst to thy death
    through grief and desire !
Thou wast a queen, and thy handmaidens wrought thee
    rich veils in their looms,
Curtained thy chamber with crimson, and strewed it
    with odorous blooms.
In the fountain that freshened thy garden warbled a
    nereid choir,
And music attended thee waking, — soft hauntings of
    flute and of lyre.
Thou wast the queen of all these, — of love, of laughter
    and song. . . .
Be glad in the summer thou makest, and memory do
    thee no wrong !

MARSYAS.

A straying flock, a mountain fold ;
A cavern arch, a well-spring cold ;
A woodland flute, a lyre of gold ;
A challenged god to contest come, a satyr overbold !

The light leaves sighed, the waters ran ;
The pupil of rough mountain Pan,
With shaggy lip and cheek of tan,
With easy breath and jocund heart the tuneful strife
        began.

His gloating eye, bent down the while,
Saw not Apollo's fateful smile, —
Saw not, from every forest aisle,
The shy and curious sylvans move in swift but noise-
        less file.

For each clear strain was drink and food
To those that dwelt within the wood ;
The dryad full-discovered stood ;
The fleeting water-spirit stayed, and backward pushed
        her hood.

And then were all consenting, save
The master-lyrist smiling grave ;
Across the strings he sudden drave
A flood of all-melodious sound, — tumultuous wave on
    wave !

And as the throbbing strings he smote,
Song rippled from his full white throat :
From cloudland bank and gulf remote
The shining ones in rapt delight were seen to glide or
    float.

That sovran sound the hills salute ;
That sovran sound brooks no dispute ;
It drowns the flute, — poor woodland flute,
That soon between the god's strong hands lies broken,
    vauntless, mute.

The strife now ended, in amaze
Doth trembling Marsyas start and gaze ;
Him, there amidst the mountain ways,
With his far-flashing golden bow, the wroth Apollo
    flays.

Beneath the cavern's jagged eaves
The hapless child of Pan he leaves,
While his warm heart, outplucked, still heaves ;
Ah, what avails it him his name to spring and river
    cleaves !

. . . .

Remember Marsyas, and beware!
The Kings of Song, — they long forbear;
They smile on us, reproof they spare,
While we, forgetful-fond, release thin reed-notes on the
air.

But they, at last, uprise in ire:
A single hand-sweep on the lyre,
A single flash of heavenly fire —
Remember Marsyas! — lo, in shame our pride and
vaunt expire!

GLAUCUS.

HEARKEN the voices of the ancient deep,
How, evermore and evermore, arise
From its unsolaced bosom moans and sighs,
That with the heart of man communion keep!
Oft dwellers by the strand awake from sleep,
Perplexed by importuning wave-borne cries;
And oft to thoughts unvoiced receive replies,
At which they weep, yet know not why they weep.

To Glaucus they have listened unaware:
He now is mighty in the mighty seas, —
Breather of rushing gale or gentle breeze,
Propitious to the toiling sailor's prayer;
And yet he once, with studious, trembling care,
Gave gifts the jealous Ocean to appease,
And from the murmuring, sea-loved, sacred trees
Wrought mast and beam, upon the deep to fare.

That hour when he from mortal frailty passed,
And all its wonder, he remembers yet:
The wine-dark water when the sun was set,
The netted fish upon the herbage cast,
The tasted plant; the leap, the billows vast,
Above his head in vaulted ceiling met;

The tridènt and the foam-flower coronet,
Wherewith the God of Waves endowed him last.

He now is subtle in all subtle lore,
The heritage of gray Poseidon's race ;
But still, half human-hearted, would retrace
His fated way, and still he haunts the shore.
Hence lives his voice through winds' and waves' uproar,
And often, for a fleeting moment's space,
Far up the beach he lays a fondling face,
And murmurs in a tongue beloved from yore.

Or now he bids the streams that hither flow
Take flowery tribute from the meadows wide,
And branch and shaft from leaning forest-side ;
He gathers all, and rocks them to and fro !
But what shall he upon the shore bestow ?
Pale-tressèd seaweeds, parted from the tide,
And shells within whose rosy crypts abide
Faint echoes of the strains the tritons blow.

Oh, yet, perchance, along the border green
That waves above the fruitless silver sands,
Its crafty leaves the magic plant expands :
But taste not, finding it, thou searcher keen !
Since grows no herb within the Sea's demesne
That could restore thee to these pleasant lands ;
Else had lamenting Glaucus broke his bands,
And slept amid the grassy hills serene.

ROSE–COLOR.

SEND me thorns a half year through,
Branches hung with frozen dew,
 Blight-leaf feuds and blanching hates,
(If ye will) ye cankered Fates :
All your leaden seasons' toil
To fair weather lends a foil !
'Gainst December how June glows, —
Hey ! the color of the rose !

Bid the morning of my day
(If ye will) be dull and gray ;
Chase afar the shining hours
With a scourge of braided showers,
Lightning-flash, and thunder-crack :
But at eve the cloudy rack
Blossoms like a garden-close, —
Hey ! the color of the rose !

Beauty, on whom homage waits,
I appeal to thee from Fates.
As my year and as my day
Genial turn from cold and gray,
Let the selfsame sign bespeak
Thy rich heart upon thy cheek.
Up the gracious June warmth goes, —
Hey ! the color of the rose !

TO-MORROW.

Is it not strange, To-morrow,
Thou hast so ill requited
Thy lover so long plighted —
Sworn not to change, To-morrow, —
Sworn not to change, — and yet,
We two have never met!
Is it not strange, To-morrow?

Where dost thou bide, To-morrow?
In depths, on heights sublime?
Where dost thou hide, To-morrow?
Past night, beyond the prime?
Art cradled with the rose,
Charm-wrapt from frosts and snows,
Through all the winter moons,
Until the south wind blows,
Till spring-tide overflows,
Till all the land is June's?
Where dost thou hide, To-morrow?
Thou callest, and I hear thee;
I haste, but come not near thee:
Where dost thou guide, To-morrow?

What largess shall I bring,
What sole and precious thing?

And how may I so serve thee
That I may all deserve thee,
And claim my own, To-morrow ?
Appoint the trysting place
Where thou wilt show thy face,
And me more tender grace
Than thou hast shown, To-morrow.
I give thee pledges, — aye,
I put in pawn To-day ;
But thou giv'st none, To-morrow.
I am too flush and free, —
To lavish all on thee !
Wilt thou atone, To-morrow ?

SONNETS.

SONNETS.

TO–DAY.

Give me health and a day, and I will make the pomp of emperors ridiculous. — EMERSON.

How rich am I to whom the Orient sends
Such gifts as yonder fair and liberal Day,
Whose argosy o'ersails the mist-bar gray,
And now its shining length of cable spends.
Upon its decks are signal-waving friends,
Who by their every jocund token say :
"Hence from thy spirit put distrust away,
This bountihood thy slackened fortune mends!
We 've olives from the soft gray trees of Peace,
And damask apples heaped for thee in sport
By the blithe Hours of young Aurora's court,
And myrrh thy heart in worship to release ;
Such freight is thine for Power's and Joy's increase ;
Oh, be no longer doubtful, — Day 's in port ! "

AFTER READING ARNOLD'S "SOHRAB AND RUSTUM."

Who reads this measure flowing strong and deep,
It seems to him old Homer's voice he hears ;
But soon grows up a sound that moves to tears, —
Tears such as Homer cannot make us weep,
Whether a grieving god bids Death and Sleep
Bear slain Sarpedon home unto his peers,
Or gray-haired Priam, kneeling, full of tears,
Seeks Hector's corse torn by the chariot's sweep.
Lightly these sorrows move us, in compare
With that which moans along the Oxus' tide,
Where by his father's hand young Sohrab died, —
Great father and great son met unaware
On Fate's dark field ; in awe we leave them there,
Wrapped in the mists that from the river glide.

(114)

MUSIC.

THE god of music dwelleth out of doors.
All seasons through his minstrelsy we meet,
Breathing by field and covert haunting-sweet:
From organ-lofts in forests old he pours
A solemn harmony; on leafy floors
To smooth autumnal pipes he moves his feet,
Or with the tingling plectrum of the sleet
In winter keen beats out his thrilling scores.
Leave me the reed unplucked beside the stream,
And he will stoop and fill it with the breeze;
Leave me the viol's frame in secret trees,
Unwrought, and it shall wake a druid theme;
Leave me the whispering shell on nereid shores:
The god of music dwelleth out of doors.

INSULATION.

So goes the world beneath thy tranquil eyes
As e'er the world has gone, with fateful speed,
Whose fierce, injurious feet take little heed
Who falls beneath them, nevermore to rise.
This neither calleth from thee tears and sighs,
Such as they give who have but power to plead,
Nor seekest thou to change by strenuous deed
The mad misrule that holds beneath the skies.
Thou art as one who, his own candle-light
And hearth-fire being pictured through the pane,
Sees not the wildness of the outer night;
For thou, forthlooking, dost but meet again
Those native things that fill thy inner sight, —
Just aims, and gentle thoughts, and honor without stain.

DESERT OR GARDEN?

ALONE; but not like that blind banished king
Who far beyond the Pharaohs' stony pile,
Amid the silent fens that drink the Nile,
Long years abode, a haggard, joyless thing,
And bade all such as sought him there to bring
A paltry gift of earth and ashes vile,
That he might build thereof a narrow isle
To mark the place of his drear sojourning. —
Alone; but not like him my days I lead,
An upland realm, not stagnant waste, my share;
Wherefore nor earth nor ashes hither bear;
But friends, if whence ye come, in wood or mead
Rise sweet and wholesome growths, bring slip and seed,
That I may set a garden fresh and fair.

(117)

TO ONE COMING.

I KNOW this pleasant breather from the south,
That seemed to have nothing to do all day
But drive the fireweed's shimmering flocks astray,
And waft along the many-colored moth, —
I know this rippling wind has not been loth
To speed thy ship where tropic calms belay;
And therefore I a singing tribute pay
The spirit that has freed thy sails from sloth.
The stars! why shine the stars so well to-night?
(Not one is absent, though of faintest ray;)
I know their steadfast lamps do guide thy way,
And thou dost lift to them thy earnest sight:
For this glad tears, quick-rushing tears, I pay —
They smile and waver in the ether height!

WINTER LEAFAGE.

EACH year I mark one lone outstanding tree,
Clad in its robings of the summer past,
Dry, wan, and shivering in the wintry blast.
It will not pay the season's rightful fee, —
It will not set its frost-burnt leafage free;
But like some palsied miser all aghast,
Who hoards his sordid treasure to the last,
It sighs, it moans, it sings in eldritch glee.
A foolish tree, to dote on summers gone ;
A faithless tree, that never feels how spring
Creeps up the world to make a leafy dawn,
And recompense for all despoilment bring !
Oh, let me not, heyday and youth withdrawn,
With failing hands to their vain semblance cling !

YOUTH AND AGE.

YOUTH, like a traveler bound through Darien,
Looks from his airy path, and each way hails
The brave delight of waves, and swollen sails
That come and go to serve shore-dwelling men.
A little space elate he fareth, then
The land swells round him, and the sea-sound fails,
And he no longer breathes the ocean gales,
Nor sees such ample sweep of sky again.
O brother travelers! though we shall not know
Reversed way through the Continent of Age,
This knowledge shall in part our grief assuage:
Still o'er the Narrow Land the free winds blow;
Its high ridge rings with songs of those who go
Bearing their undepleted heritage.

(120)

LOVE'S SOLITUDE AND SOCIETY.

WHEN I must go into the turmoil rude
Of worldly men and ways, I cheerly go,
Since there I am as one that hath no foe,
But moves in sylvan peace, where boughs exclude
The too fierce sun, and paths with leaves are strewed,
And bird-sought brooks in shady stillness flow:
I need not shun the turmoil, since I know
That Love will make for me sweet solitude.
And if I into exile must be sent,
Let me not grieve; the Fate's commanding lips
I kiss, and take my way without a fear.
If in the desert I must pitch my tent,
Love hath within itself all fellowships, —
Is friends, and home, and rest, and plenteous cheer.

CONSTANCY.

I AM not constant as yon constant rocks,
That have their bases under ocean's floor,
That yield no piteous span, receive no score,
Though ships make thither, waves deal shocks on
      shocks.
I am but constant as the sea, whose flocks,
How wide soe'er they wander, evermore
Morning and evening crowd the vacant shore,
At beck of her who smiles through silvery locks ;
Constant, but as the oak now bare and dry,
That soon the genial season shall restore,
And its gray arms with fluttering honors fill ;
Or as the violet, that seems to die,
Yet can its azure angel raise it still,
To greet the coming springtime as before.

THE HEART OF SUMMER.

THE heart of Summer — find me where it beats !
Search through the dawn-bright chambers of the rose ;
Ay, question every tender breeze that blows
From off the water-lily's naiad fleets.
Oh, not with these !   Then bide till later heats
Lead forth the poppy, that doth lead repose ;
Watch narrowly when at the day's faint close
Its sovran hour the evening-primrose greets.
Thou Summer's lover !   Yet for all thy care
She will not show to thee her secret heart.
Though now its throbbings take the languid air,
And now a flush across the fields will start,
And now full near she breathes, soon otherwhere,
Mindless of thee, she moves and dwells apart.

NILUS.

WHAT springs feed that great vein that from the heart
Of searchless Ethiopia descends,
That makes the changes of the year, and lends
A springtide to the land dim-faced and swart;
Whether it moves with foamy plunge and start,
Shaking its reed-built isles, or smoothly bends
Round Morn-loved Memnon's slumber, and befriends
The scarrèd Sphinx that sits her throne apart!
Now hear we, rising from the spacious land,
A murmur as of builders in the sun ;
Or now, on some Canopian palace-roof,
With old diviners of the stars we stand,
While through the dusk the glimmering waters run,
Like some long caravan winding aloof.

(124)

THE END OF THE WORLD.

Thou threat'nest that the world shall be undone,
And true thou sayest, seer of evil, true,
Though they that hearken to thy voice be few.
Even yesterday the ruin was begun,
Runs on to-day, and shall to-morrow run :
The world does end whene'er the wondrous clue
Of life is snapped, and some one sighs adieu
To all beneath the long-surviving sun.
And there are those of mortals sojourning
Who smile when they thy dismal burden hear,
Because thou warnest of a forepast thing.
Hope is behind them, and Hope's vexer, Fear ;
The world is ended, and with idle swing
Is driven on, a wrecked, unlighted sphere !

AUTUMN.

'T IS now that spiders in the casement weave,
Or launch their silken air-ships on the breeze;
'T is now that honey-ripeness feeds the bees
Where vine-borne amber sweets their prison cleave,
And golden spheres their leafy heavens leave.
The same wind whispers through the orchard trees
That blew our swallows over southern seas,
And stole the robin's vesper from our eve.
The spirit of the year, like bacchant crowned,
With lighted torch goes careless on his way;
And soon bursts into flame the maple's spray,
And vines are running fire along the ground.
But softly! on October's blazing bound
How laugh the violet eyes of tender May!

THE INTERPRETER.

OH, well these places knew and loved us twain!
The genii softly laughed to see us pass,
To kiss our blessed hands up climbed the grass,
And on our pathway danced a flowery train;
To counsel us each agèd tree was fain,
And all its leafy accents we could class;
By symbol-circles on its polished glass,
By chiming shallows, still the brook spake plain.
Now all is changed: I look and list in vain;
As one who sits and hears a solemn mass,
In other language, in an alien fane,
So I without thee in these haunts, alas!
Am Nature's stranger, — so must I remain
Till, sweet interpreter! thou come again.

A MESSENGER.

A TRUSTY messenger I straight would find,
That knows all airy routes without a guide,
That has long years in Love's employ been tried,
Has done keen spiritings from mind to mind,
And still will be sweet-spoken, deft, and kind . . . .
Now haste, and come where my Desired doth bide,
Past many a stripped and moaning forest-side
Within the chiefdom of the Northern Wind.
When sails aloft the thistle's downy sphere,
Tell her, as many as its plumules are,
So many are the thoughts I send by thee;
Tell her, when summerward the swallows steer,
Love does not so, but by the magnet star
Aims north his flight, and will no laggard be !

GRIEF'S STRATAGEM.

In Helen's house (Ulysses counted dead)
The hearts of all by sorrow's wave were swept,
And host and guests, unshamed, together wept,
Yet wept not all for great Ulysses sped:
Though plenteous tears the youth from Pylos shed,
Seizing the tearful chance like grief's adept,
He mourned his own, his brother dear, who slept
Where hostile soil with best Greek blood was fed.
Thus I — if fortune would so far befriend
To hither bring some spirit scourgèd sore,
Some wrong that loudly knocks at pity's door —
Might seem in charity those tears to spend,
That otherwise I dare not let descend
To ease my heart of grief's occulted store !

THE RETURN TO NATURE.

O NATURE, take me home, and henceforth keep!
Laugh out at me with all thy mirthful streams,
To break the tenor of dull-hearted dreams;
From ambush in a waving thicket leap,
And startle with a song as past I creep;
Or speed me by invisible wild teams
That drive through forests and rough mountain-seams,
And furrow dark the forehead of the deep.
Nay, do thou more for me, great griefless friend!
Hurt to the core, without the gift to weep,
Back from man's world to thine I groping tend;
Now let thy clods unkindled smoothly sweep
This cooling clod — my heart; then do thou bend,
Uplift, and in bright calm my spirit steep.

R. W. GILDER'S "THE NEW DAY."

ALL books that for Love's sake are ever penned
Live creatures are, and from their being's date
Have their good genii, watchful of their fate,
To speed the heartward errand, and to lend
An affluent touch that doth all art transcend.
Sometimes it falls to readers' rich estate
That they behold these spirits consecrate,
As they upon their chosen cares attend.
Thus saw I these rare leaves, surnamed of Dawn,
Fresh smitten by a rosy eastern beam,
And, midmost in its flushing, something white
With lucent dewy wings enfolding drawn :
Young Eros of the Greek's supernal dream
To guard his own came down in native light !

(131)

STRENGTH.

A SECRET thing is Strength! The strongest wear
No steely harness for the breast or head :
Address of gossamer, their raiment shred,
Were all as proof to them ; unarmed they dare
Advance where sworded legions would despair.
They ne'er are hunger-bitten, but are fed
On unknown miracles of meat and bread,
And rock-pent sluices issue at their prayer.
A secret thing is Strength, that without sleight
The glooming wrath of Fate they can appease ;
For lo! they are not conscious of their might
More than the winds that blow, or moving seas,
Or planets circling in eternal light ;
And all their deeds seem wrought with rhythmic ease.

TO THE DEAD.

I. TO ALL.

WE say ye sleep, but light your sleep, meseems ;
We call ye silent, when your undertone
Threads all this world's exultance, wrath, and moan,
Ye lifeful dead, with whom this sad earth teems !
Are these your voices mixed with troubled streams ?
Is this your speech, in ancient tongues unknown,
Through twilight fields and darkling wood-ways blown ?
Have ye the winds of heaven to serve your schemes ?
O aye-increasing, far outnumbering host,
Crowd not so close our handful breathing clan :
This moment ye are distant but a span,
Such as Ulysses kept on that stern coast
Where round the warm libation, lips all wan,
With clamor shrill, came many a thirsting ghost !

II. TO ONE.

Thou movest in their front, serene, serene !
How smilest thou, as one not knowing yet
That he is Death's, — the rose and violet
(Not asphodel) about thy temples seen !

(133)

Now with drawn spirit-sword I stand between
Thee and the murmuring shades that so beset :
Be thy lips only with the offering wet ;
Then speak ! — where goest thou ? where hast thou
    been ?
In vain, in vain ! for, wavering through the gloom,
Thou art become stream, forest, hill . . . and now
It is the evening star that masks thy brow.
Gone art thou, gone the rose and violet bloom,
And the unnumbered shades their sway resume :
Shall all the dead speak to me — and not thou !

III.

What if in truth the heaven where thou art
Rests its pure sapphire base upon these hills
Where thy late paths a green oblivion fills ?
If from a window where the moist clouds part
Thou dost look forth and watch new beauty start
Beneath the April rain by plashing rills,
Or if above far fields those sun-warm thrills
Are the rich fervor of thy lifted heart ?
What though all this be true ? — it can but prove
Thou dost companion Nature as of old :
Then, also Love's, thou wast not far to seek,
A sigh could break thy thought's utmost remove ;
Now, ever silent, thou thy way dost hold, —
Would I might know that thou desir'st to speak !

IV.

One saith who knew thee well, who loved thee true,
Thou art to him an influence benign, —
Like gentlest wind in a close grove of pine,
Known but by sound and fragrance breathed there-
  through.
Another saith he feels thee draw the clue
Thou here didst hold with us, — a soul divine,
A thing of light, and blent with day's clear shine,
While we 'mid thinning darkness still pursue.
Thy lesser loves have cheer; but what to me
Who loved thee most, whom thou didst love past all,—
Hast thou no voice to send across the deep ?
No voice I hear, — I turn to God from thee :
God's pity ! when Death's sundering blow doth fall
Do greatest loves the strictest silence keep ?

MIGRATION.

THE cagèd bird, that all the autumn day
In quiet dwells, when falls the autumn eve
Seeks how its liberty it may achieve,
Beats at the wires and its poor wings doth fray:
For now desire of migrant change holds sway;
This summer-vacant land it longs to leave,
While its free peers on tireless pinions cleave
The haunted twilight, speeding south their way.
Not otherwise than as the prisoned bird,
We here dwell careless of our captive state
Until light dwindles, and the year grows late,
And answering note to note no more is heard;
Then, our loved fellows flown, the soul is stirred
To follow them where summer has no date.

www.ingramcontent.com/pod-product-compliance
Lightning Source LLC
Chambersburg PA
CBHW030609270326
41927CB00007B/1102